Micheal J. Saylor present and future crytocurrency prediction

The Visionary Investor

Harold Muller

All rights reserved. No part of this publication may be reproduced, distributed, or transmitted in any form or by any means, including photocopying, recording, or other electronic or mechanical methods, without the prior written permission of the publisher, except in the case of brief quotations embodied in critical reviews and certain other noncommercial uses permitted by copyright law.

Copyright © 2024 by Harold Muller

Table of content

Introduction..6
    Who is Michael J. Saylor?.. 6
    His Journey from MicroStrategy to Bitcoin Evangelism.. 8
    Why His Bitcoin Predictions Matter in the Crypto and Financial World... 11

Chapter One: The Bitcoin Revolution.........................14
    Overview of Bitcoin's rise as a digital asset............ 14
    Key Milestones in Bitcoin's History and Adoption... 16
    The Role of Decentralization and Digital Scarcity...19

Chapter Two: Michael J. Saylor's Bitcoin Journey. 23
    How Saylor transitioned to becoming a major Bitcoin advocate.. 23
    MicroStrategy's Investment Strategy and Its Influence on Corporate Adoption............................ 25
    Saylor's Public Stance on Bitcoin's Role as Digital Gold.. 27

Chapter Three: The $100K Prediction for 2025........31
    Analysis of Saylor's $100K prediction for Bitcoin by 2025.. 31
    Analysis of Saylor's $100K Prediction for Bitcoin by 2025.. 31
    Factors He Believes Will Drive This Growth........... 33
    Key Quotes and Interviews Supporting His Vision. 36

Chapter Four: The Path to $1 Million........................39
    Saylor's Long-Term Projection of Bitcoin Reaching

$1M...........39
The Role of Scarcity (21 Million Cap) and Increasing Demand........... 41
Comparisons to Gold and Other Stores of Value....44

Chapter 5: Bitcoin's Volatility—A Necessary Growth Element...........48
Saylor's Perspective on Volatility as an Essential Part of Bitcoin's Evolution........... 48
Case Studies of Major Price Swings and Their Impact on the Market........... 51
Insights on Managing Risks in Bitcoin Investments 55

Chapter Six: The Institutional Revolution........... 58
Analysis of Institutional Bitcoin Adoption: ETFs and Corporate Investments........... 58
The Influence of Major Players like BlackRock and Fidelity........... 62
How Institutions Align with Saylor's Vision........... 65

Chapter Seven: The Future of Bitcoin Under Global Changes........... 69
Bitcoin's Potential in a Changing Political and Economic Landscape........... 69
How New U.S. Crypto Policies Could Affect Saylor's Predictions...........74
Global Adoption Trends and Their Alignment with Saylor's Foresight........... 77

Chapter Eight: Criticism and Alternative Views...... 80
Addressing Skepticism Surrounding Saylor's Predictions........... 81
Exploring Bearish Perspectives on Bitcoin's Future... 85
Balancing Optimism with Caution........... 88

Conclusion..**90**
    Saylor's Broader Philosophy on Bitcoin as a
    Transformative Technology........................ 90
    Final Thoughts on Saylor's Predictions and Their
    Significance in the Digital Economy........................95

Introduction

Who is Michael J. Saylor?

Michael J. Saylor is a trailblazing entrepreneur, author, and one of the most influential figures in the cryptocurrency space. Born on February 4, 1965, in Lincoln, Nebraska, Saylor demonstrated early academic prowess that set the stage for his remarkable career. He graduated as the valedictorian of his high school class and pursued a degree in Aeronautics and Astronautics at the Massachusetts Institute of Technology (MIT), one of the most prestigious engineering schools in the world. At MIT, Saylor also earned a double major in science, technology, and society, highlighting his multifaceted intellectual interests.

Saylor's career took off in 1989 when he co-founded MicroStrategy, a company that specialized in software and business intelligence. Under his leadership as CEO, MicroStrategy grew into a global powerhouse, offering analytics solutions to Fortune 500 companies. Saylor's visionary leadership was evident in his ability to foresee technological trends, such as the rise of mobile computing and the need for data-driven decision-making.

However, Saylor's journey has not been without challenges. In 2000, MicroStrategy faced a financial scandal involving the misreporting of earnings, which led to a sharp decline in the company's stock value. Despite these setbacks, Saylor remained resilient, steering the company back to stability and profitability. This period of professional hardship shaped his ability to take calculated risks and think long-term qualities that would later define his approach to Bitcoin.

In the 2010s, Saylor began questioning the sustainability of traditional financial systems. As inflation eroded the purchasing power of fiat currencies, he sought a solution that could preserve value over time. This quest led him to Bitcoin, a decentralized digital currency that operates on a transparent and immutable blockchain. Saylor's transition from a software executive to a Bitcoin evangelist was not just a personal evolution; it marked a turning point for the entire cryptocurrency industry.

His Journey from MicroStrategy to Bitcoin Evangelism

Michael J. Saylor's shift from leading a business intelligence software firm to becoming one of the most prominent advocates for Bitcoin is a story of adaptability and foresight. In 2020, as the global economy grappled with the effects of the COVID-19 pandemic, Saylor began to reevaluate MicroStrategy's corporate treasury strategy. Traditionally, companies held their reserves in cash or cash equivalents, but Saylor recognized the risks associated with fiat currency. Central banks worldwide were engaging in aggressive monetary expansion, leading to concerns about inflation and currency devaluation.

Faced with the challenge of preserving shareholder value, Saylor decided to take a bold step. In August 2020, MicroStrategy announced that it had purchased $250 million worth of Bitcoin, making it the first publicly traded company to adopt Bitcoin as a primary treasury reserve asset. This move was unprecedented and controversial, sparking debates in financial and tech circles. Many viewed it as a high-risk gamble, but Saylor saw it as a necessary hedge against inflation and a strategic investment in the future of money.

Saylor's conviction was rooted in extensive research and analysis. He studied Bitcoin's fundamental properties: its capped supply of 21 million coins, its decentralized nature, and its growing adoption as digital gold. Unlike fiat currencies, which can be printed at will by central banks, Bitcoin's scarcity made it a reliable store of value. Saylor compared Bitcoin to historical stores of value like gold and real estate, arguing that Bitcoin was superior due to its portability, divisibility, and verifiability.

MicroStrategy's initial Bitcoin purchase was just the beginning. Over the following months, the company continued to accumulate Bitcoin, eventually acquiring billions of dollars' worth of the cryptocurrency. This aggressive strategy transformed MicroStrategy into a de facto Bitcoin investment vehicle, with its stock price closely correlated to Bitcoin's performance. Saylor personally invested in Bitcoin as well, acquiring hundreds of millions of dollars' worth of the cryptocurrency with his own funds.

As Saylor became more vocal about his Bitcoin strategy, he emerged as a leading voice in the crypto community. He published detailed essays and gave numerous interviews explaining the rationale behind his decisions. He framed Bitcoin not just as an investment but as a moral imperative in the face of what he called "fiat currency debasement." Saylor's advocacy extended beyond MicroStrategy; he founded the Bitcoin Mining Council to address environmental concerns and promote sustainable mining practices.

His evangelism also had a ripple effect on institutional adoption. Saylor's endorsement lent credibility to Bitcoin, encouraging other CEOs and institutional investors to consider the cryptocurrency. Companies like Tesla and Square followed MicroStrategy's lead by adding Bitcoin to their balance sheets. By framing Bitcoin as a solution to macroeconomic challenges, Saylor bridged the gap between the crypto world and traditional finance, making Bitcoin more accessible and appealing to a broader audience.

Why His Bitcoin Predictions Matter in the Crypto and Financial World

Michael J. Saylor's Bitcoin predictions carry significant weight because of his unique position at the intersection of technology, finance, and macroeconomics. As a seasoned entrepreneur with a track record of identifying transformative trends, Saylor's insights are not mere speculation,they are grounded in data, historical analysis, and a deep understanding of market dynamics.

Saylor's prediction that Bitcoin could reach $100,000 by 2025 and eventually $1 million is rooted in several key factors:

1. Scarcity and Demand: Bitcoin's fixed supply of 21 million coins makes it inherently scarce. As more individuals, institutions, and even governments adopt Bitcoin, demand is expected to outpace supply, driving up the price.

2. Institutional Adoption: Saylor has been instrumental in accelerating institutional interest in Bitcoin. He argues that as more companies and financial institutions

recognize Bitcoin's value as a store of wealth, the influx of capital will create a virtuous cycle of growth.

3. Macroeconomic Trends: Saylor believes that Bitcoin's rise is inevitable in the face of inflation, currency devaluation, and geopolitical instability. As central banks continue to expand money supplies, he sees Bitcoin as a safe haven for preserving wealth.

4. Technological Advancements: Innovations in the Bitcoin ecosystem, such as the Lightning Network for faster transactions and improved scalability, further enhance its utility and adoption potential.

Saylor's predictions are significant because they challenge conventional narratives about Bitcoin. Critics often dismiss Bitcoin as a speculative asset or a bubble, but Saylor presents it as a long-term solution to systemic economic problems. By articulating a clear and compelling case for Bitcoin, he has helped shift the perception of cryptocurrencies from fringe assets to legitimate investment vehicles.

Moreover, Saylor's predictions have practical implications for investors, policymakers, and businesses. If Bitcoin were to reach $100,000 or $1 million, it would fundamentally alter the financial landscape, creating new opportunities and challenges. For investors, it represents a chance to participate in a historic wealth creation event. For policymakers, it raises questions about regulation, taxation, and the role of decentralized currencies in a centralized financial system.

Saylor's influence extends beyond his predictions; it lies in his ability to inspire action. Through his writings, speeches, and leadership, he has galvanized a movement of Bitcoin believers who share his vision of a decentralized, borderless financial system. Whether his predictions come true or not, Saylor's advocacy has already left an indelible mark on the crypto and financial worlds.

Chapter One: The Bitcoin Revolution

Overview of Bitcoin's rise as a digital asset.

Bitcoin's rise as a digital asset has been nothing short of revolutionary, marking a paradigm shift in how individuals, corporations, and governments perceive money and value. Created in 2009 by an anonymous entity known as Satoshi Nakamoto, Bitcoin emerged as a response to the global financial crisis of 2008. At the time, trust in traditional financial institutions was at an all-time low, and the world was searching for alternatives to centralized systems that were prone to failure and corruption. Bitcoin answered this call by introducing a decentralized form of currency based on blockchain technology.

Bitcoin is not just a currency; it is a system that redefines the principles of finance. Built on transparency, security, and immutability, Bitcoin operates without a central authority, relying instead on a network of participants who validate and secure transactions. This decentralization gives Bitcoin its unique strength, offering a stark contrast to fiat currencies controlled by governments and central banks.

In its early years, Bitcoin was largely confined to the fringes of the internet, attracting tech enthusiasts, libertarians, and cryptography experts. It was used primarily for niche transactions, such as purchasing goods on platforms like Silk Road, an online black market. However, as its underlying technology became better understood, Bitcoin began to shed its controversial image and gain traction as a legitimate digital asset.

The turning point came when people realized Bitcoin's potential as a store of value, similar to gold. Unlike fiat currencies, which can be printed in unlimited quantities, Bitcoin has a capped supply of 21 million coins, making it inherently scarce. This digital scarcity, combined with its global accessibility and resistance to censorship, positioned Bitcoin as an attractive asset for individuals seeking to hedge against inflation and economic uncertainty.

Today, Bitcoin is widely regarded as the flagship cryptocurrency, with a market capitalization that often exceeds $1 trillion during bullish periods. It is no longer just a speculative asset; it is a tool for financial empowerment, enabling millions of people worldwide to participate in a decentralized economy. From remittances and microtransactions to institutional investments and national adoption, Bitcoin has evolved into a multifaceted asset that continues to disrupt traditional finance.

Key Milestones in Bitcoin's History and Adoption

Bitcoin's journey from a white paper to a global phenomenon is marked by several key milestones that underscore its growing influence and adoption.

1. The Genesis Block (2009):
On January 3, 2009, Satoshi Nakamoto mined the first Bitcoin block, known as the Genesis Block. Embedded in the block's code was a message referencing a newspaper headline about the financial crisis: "The Times 03/Jan/2009 Chancellor on brink of second bailout for banks." This message symbolized Bitcoin's mission to offer an alternative to the failing traditional financial system.

2. The First Bitcoin Transaction (2010):
In May 2010, Laszlo Hanyecz made the first documented Bitcoin transaction by purchasing two pizzas for 10,000 BTC. This event, now celebrated annually as Bitcoin Pizza Day, highlighted Bitcoin's use as a medium of exchange, though its value was still minuscule at the time.

3. Bitcoin Reaches $1 (2011):
Bitcoin's value reached $1 for the first time in February 2011, marking a significant milestone in its journey

toward mainstream recognition. This achievement demonstrated that Bitcoin could hold real-world value and sparked growing interest among early adopters.

4. The Rise of Exchanges (2010–2013):
The creation of cryptocurrency exchanges like Mt. Gox and Coinbase played a pivotal role in Bitcoin's adoption. These platforms made it easier for individuals to buy, sell, and trade Bitcoin, increasing its accessibility and liquidity. However, the collapse of Mt. Gox in 2014, following a massive hack, underscored the need for secure and trustworthy platforms.

5. Mainstream Media Attention (2013–2017):
Bitcoin began to capture mainstream media attention as its price surged and more people became aware of its potential. High-profile endorsements, such as those from tech entrepreneurs and financial experts, further legitimized Bitcoin in the public eye.

6. Institutional Adoption (2020–2021):
The involvement of institutional investors marked a turning point in Bitcoin's history. Companies like MicroStrategy, Tesla, and Square began adding Bitcoin to their balance sheets, while investment firms launched Bitcoin-focused funds and ETFs. This wave of institutional adoption significantly boosted Bitcoin's credibility and market capitalization.

7. National Adoption (2021):
In 2021, El Salvador became the first country to adopt Bitcoin as legal tender, a historic moment that underscored its potential as a national currency. Other countries have since explored similar initiatives, signaling a growing acceptance of Bitcoin on a global scale.

8. Bitcoin's All-Time High (2021):
Bitcoin reached an all-time high of over $68,000 in November 2021, solidifying its status as a leading financial asset. This milestone was driven by increasing adoption, favorable regulatory developments, and growing interest from retail and institutional investors.

The Role of Decentralization and Digital Scarcity

Two fundamental principles underpin Bitcoin's success: decentralization and digital scarcity. These concepts set Bitcoin apart from traditional currencies and make it a revolutionary force in the financial world.

1. Decentralization:
Decentralization is the cornerstone of Bitcoin's architecture. Unlike traditional financial systems, which

rely on centralized authorities like banks and governments, Bitcoin operates on a peer-to-peer network. This network is maintained by thousands of nodes distributed across the globe, each of which validates and records transactions on the blockchain.

The decentralized nature of Bitcoin ensures that no single entity has control over the network. This makes it resistant to censorship, fraud, and manipulation. For example, while governments can freeze bank accounts or devalue currencies, they cannot alter Bitcoin's blockchain or confiscate funds stored in a Bitcoin wallet without the owner's private keys.

Decentralization also enhances Bitcoin's security. By distributing the network's operations across multiple nodes, Bitcoin eliminates single points of failure, reducing the risk of hacks and system failures. This decentralized model has inspired countless other blockchain projects and has become a defining feature of the cryptocurrency ecosystem.

2. Digital Scarcity:

Digital scarcity is another revolutionary aspect of Bitcoin. Traditional currencies are subject to inflation because central banks can print unlimited amounts of money. In contrast, Bitcoin has a fixed supply of 21 million coins, a cap hard-coded into its protocol. This finite supply ensures that Bitcoin cannot be devalued through excessive issuance, making it a reliable store of value.

Bitcoin's scarcity is further reinforced by its issuance schedule. New Bitcoins are introduced into circulation through a process called mining, which involves solving complex mathematical problems to validate transactions and secure the network. Every four years, the reward for mining is halved in an event known as the halving. This reduces the rate at which new Bitcoins are created, gradually decreasing the supply over time.

The combination of fixed supply and declining issuance creates a deflationary dynamic, where Bitcoin becomes more valuable as demand increases. This contrasts sharply with inflationary fiat currencies, whose purchasing power diminishes over time.

Digital scarcity also has psychological and economic implications. The knowledge that only 21 million Bitcoins will ever exist creates a sense of urgency among investors, driving demand and fostering long-term holding behavior. This has contributed to Bitcoin's reputation as "digital gold" and its adoption as a store of value.

Bitcoin's rise as a digital asset is a story of innovation, resilience, and vision. From its humble beginnings as an experiment in decentralization to its current status as a global financial phenomenon, Bitcoin has redefined what money can be. By leveraging the principles of decentralization and digital scarcity, it has created a new financial paradigm that challenges traditional systems and empowers individuals.

Chapter Two: Michael J. Saylor's Bitcoin Journey

How Saylor transitioned to becoming a major Bitcoin advocate.

Michael J. Saylor's transformation from a tech entrepreneur and CEO to one of Bitcoin's most vocal proponents is a remarkable story of vision, adaptation, and conviction. Before his Bitcoin advocacy, Saylor was best known as the co-founder and CEO of MicroStrategy, a leading business intelligence and software company he established in 1989. For decades, his focus was on building cutting-edge software solutions for enterprises, which earned MicroStrategy a solid reputation in the tech industry.

However, a series of global economic challenges and personal realizations led Saylor to re-evaluate his approach to wealth preservation and corporate strategy. In 2020, the world was grappling with the COVID-19 pandemic, which not only disrupted economies but also triggered unprecedented monetary expansion. Central banks around the globe responded to the economic crisis by printing trillions of dollars to stimulate growth, raising concerns about inflation and the declining value of fiat currencies.

Saylor, like many business leaders, began to worry about the impact of inflation on MicroStrategy's cash reserves, which were traditionally held in U.S. dollars. In a world where fiat currencies seemed increasingly unstable, he sought an asset that could serve as a reliable store of value. His search led him to Bitcoin.

Saylor's journey into Bitcoin wasn't a spur-of-the-moment decision. He immersed himself in understanding the technology, its underlying principles, and its potential to disrupt traditional finance. Saylor's background in science and engineering enabled him to grasp Bitcoin's core features, including decentralization, digital scarcity, and security. He quickly realized that Bitcoin was more than just a cryptocurrency, it was a revolutionary monetary network.

In interviews, Saylor often describes Bitcoin as "the apex property of the human race" and likens it to digital real estate. For Saylor, Bitcoin represented a chance to preserve and grow wealth in a world where fiat money was rapidly losing purchasing power. By mid-2020, he had become convinced that Bitcoin was not just a speculative investment but a necessity for individuals, corporations, and even nations seeking financial security. This conviction marked the beginning of Saylor's transition into a major Bitcoin advocate. Unlike many corporate executives who adopt Bitcoin cautiously,

Saylor embraced it with unbridled enthusiasm. He began publicly discussing Bitcoin's potential to reshape the global financial system, positioning himself as a thought leader in the space.

MicroStrategy's Investment Strategy and Its Influence on Corporate Adoption

One of the most significant moments in Michael Saylor's Bitcoin journey was MicroStrategy's decision to adopt Bitcoin as its primary treasury asset. In August 2020, MicroStrategy announced its first purchase of 21,454 Bitcoins, worth $250 million at the time. This move was groundbreaking, as it marked the first instance of a publicly traded company using Bitcoin to hedge against inflation and economic uncertainty.

The decision was not without risk. Critics questioned the wisdom of allocating such a large portion of the company's cash reserves to a volatile and relatively new asset. However, Saylor was undeterred. He viewed Bitcoin as a superior store of value compared to traditional options like bonds, gold, or fiat currencies.

Over the next several months, MicroStrategy doubled down on its Bitcoin strategy, acquiring additional coins through direct purchases and debt offerings. By the end of 2021, the company held over 120,000 Bitcoins, making it one of the largest corporate holders of the cryptocurrency. This aggressive accumulation strategy earned MicroStrategy significant media attention and set a precedent for other corporations to consider Bitcoin as a strategic asset.

MicroStrategy's Bitcoin strategy also had a profound impact on its stock price and investor sentiment. While the company's core business remained steady, its Bitcoin holdings became a key driver of shareholder value. MicroStrategy's stock price surged, attracting both institutional and retail investors who wanted exposure to Bitcoin without directly holding the cryptocurrency.

Saylor's bold approach influenced other companies to explore Bitcoin as a treasury asset. Square (now Block), Tesla, and other firms followed MicroStrategy's lead, adding Bitcoin to their balance sheets. Saylor also spearheaded educational initiatives, such as the Bitcoin for Corporations conference, where he shared insights into MicroStrategy's strategy and provided resources for other executives interested in adopting Bitcoin.

Beyond corporate adoption, MicroStrategy's Bitcoin strategy highlighted the broader implications of Bitcoin as a financial asset. Saylor argued that Bitcoin's decentralized and deflationary nature made it an ideal tool for preserving wealth in an increasingly uncertain economic environment. By framing Bitcoin as a solution to the challenges of inflation and currency devaluation,

Saylor helped shift the narrative around cryptocurrency from speculation to utility.

Saylor's Public Stance on Bitcoin's Role as Digital Gold

Michael Saylor's advocacy for Bitcoin is rooted in his belief that it is the digital equivalent of gold, but vastly superior in nearly every respect. For centuries, gold has been considered the ultimate store of value due to its scarcity, durability, and universal acceptance. However, Saylor argues that Bitcoin improves upon gold's properties, making it the "hardest money" ever created.

One of Saylor's key arguments is that Bitcoin's supply is fixed at 21 million coins, whereas the supply of gold is subject to gradual increases through mining. This fixed supply creates true digital scarcity, ensuring that Bitcoin's value is not diluted over time. In contrast, gold's annual production, while limited, introduces a small but continuous inflationary effect.

Another advantage of Bitcoin over gold is its portability and divisibility. Gold is heavy, difficult to transport, and expensive to secure. Bitcoin, on the other hand, exists entirely in digital form, making it easy to transfer across borders at the speed of the internet. Moreover, Bitcoin is highly divisible, with each coin divisible into 100 million units (satoshis), enabling transactions of any size.

Saylor also emphasizes Bitcoin's resistance to confiscation and censorship. Gold, being a physical asset, is vulnerable to seizure by governments or theft by individuals. Bitcoin's decentralized nature and cryptographic security make it nearly impossible for external parties to confiscate or censor without the owner's private keys.

For Saylor, Bitcoin's role as digital gold extends beyond individual wealth preservation. He believes it has the potential to become a global reserve asset, replacing traditional stores of value like gold and government bonds. In his view, Bitcoin's adoption as a reserve asset would create a more stable and transparent financial system, reducing reliance on centralized institutions prone to corruption and mismanagement.

Saylor's public stance on Bitcoin as digital gold has made him a polarizing figure in the financial world. While supporters praise his visionary outlook and unwavering commitment, critics argue that his views are overly optimistic and fail to account for Bitcoin's volatility and regulatory challenges. Nevertheless, Saylor remains steadfast in his belief that Bitcoin is the most important financial innovation of the 21st century.

To promote this vision, Saylor has appeared on numerous podcasts, interviews, and conferences, sharing his insights on Bitcoin's potential to transform the global economy. He often describes Bitcoin as a "monetary energy network" that transcends borders and empowers individuals to achieve financial independence.

Michael Saylor's Bitcoin journey is a testament to his willingness to embrace change and challenge conventional thinking. From his initial skepticism to becoming one of Bitcoin's most vocal advocates, Saylor's transformation underscores the transformative power of this digital asset. Through his leadership at MicroStrategy and his tireless advocacy, he has played a pivotal role in advancing Bitcoin's adoption and shaping the future of finance.

Chapter Three: The $100K Prediction for 2025

Analysis of Saylor's $100K prediction for Bitcoin by 2025.

Michael J. Saylor's prediction that Bitcoin will reach $100,000 by 2025 has sparked intrigue, debate, and optimism within the cryptocurrency community and beyond. As a leading voice in Bitcoin advocacy, Saylor's forecast is not just a numerical target; it reflects a comprehensive understanding of Bitcoin's potential as a transformative asset in a rapidly evolving financial ecosystem. This chapter delves into his $100K prediction, exploring the factors he believes will drive this growth and the key insights he has shared in support of his vision.

Analysis of Saylor's $100K Prediction for Bitcoin by 2025

Saylor's $100,000 prediction for Bitcoin by 2025 is rooted in his deep conviction that the cryptocurrency is poised for significant growth as a global store of value. His forecast is not based on speculation but on an analytical approach that considers Bitcoin's unique attributes, macroeconomic trends, and shifting attitudes toward digital assets.

Saylor often compares Bitcoin to gold, arguing that it is the digital successor to the precious metal. According to him, Bitcoin's fixed supply of 21 million coins and its decentralized nature make it the hardest and most predictable monetary asset ever created. In this context, Bitcoin's market capitalization, which has hovered between $500 billion and $1 trillion in recent years, is seen as vastly undervalued compared to gold's $12 trillion market cap. Saylor believes that as Bitcoin continues to gain acceptance as digital gold, its price will naturally rise, potentially reaching $100,000 in the near term.

Saylor's prediction is also informed by Bitcoin's adoption curve. Drawing parallels to the adoption of the internet in the 1990s and early 2000s, Saylor sees Bitcoin as being in a similar phase of exponential growth. He highlights the increasing number of individuals, institutions, and governments recognizing Bitcoin's potential as a hedge against inflation, a tool for financial sovereignty, and a superior alternative to traditional assets.

In interviews, Saylor frequently emphasizes that Bitcoin is not just a speculative investment but a necessity for anyone seeking to protect their wealth in an era of rampant monetary expansion. He argues that the world is facing an unprecedented wave of currency devaluation, and Bitcoin offers a lifeboat for those looking to escape the sinking ship of fiat money.

Factors He Believes Will Drive This Growth

Michael Saylor has outlined several key factors that he believes will propel Bitcoin to $100,000 by 2025. These include institutional adoption, regulatory clarity, and geopolitical trends. Each of these factors plays a critical role in shaping Bitcoin's trajectory and underscores its potential as a revolutionary asset.

1. Institutional Adoption

One of the most significant drivers of Bitcoin's growth, according to Saylor, is the increasing adoption of Bitcoin by institutional investors. Over the past few years, large corporations, asset managers, and even pension funds have begun to recognize Bitcoin's value proposition as a store of value and a hedge against inflation.
Saylor's own company, MicroStrategy, has led the way in demonstrating how Bitcoin can be integrated into corporate treasury strategies. By converting the company's cash reserves into Bitcoin, Saylor has set a precedent for other corporations to follow. Tesla, Block (formerly Square), and other firms have also made

substantial Bitcoin investments, signaling a broader trend of institutional interest.

Moreover, the launch of Bitcoin ETFs (Exchange-Traded Funds) in various countries has made it easier for institutional and retail investors to gain exposure to Bitcoin. Saylor believes that as more financial products tied to Bitcoin become available, the demand for the cryptocurrency will increase, driving its price higher.

2. Regulatory Clarity

Another critical factor driving Saylor's $100K prediction is the gradual emergence of regulatory clarity in the cryptocurrency space. In its early years, Bitcoin faced significant skepticism and regulatory uncertainty, which hindered its adoption. However, recent developments indicate a growing acceptance of Bitcoin by governments and regulatory bodies.

For instance, countries like the United States have begun to lay the groundwork for clearer rules around cryptocurrency taxation, trading, and custody. While some regulations may impose restrictions, Saylor argues that regulatory clarity will ultimately benefit Bitcoin by reducing uncertainty and fostering trust among institutional investors.

In addition, the recognition of Bitcoin as legal tender in countries like El Salvador has further legitimized its role as a global financial asset. Saylor believes that as more nations explore Bitcoin's potential as a monetary tool, its adoption will accelerate, pushing its price toward the $100K mark.

3. Geopolitical Trends

Geopolitical developments are another major driver of Bitcoin's growth, according to Saylor. In an increasingly interconnected and uncertain world, Bitcoin offers a unique solution to challenges such as currency instability, capital controls, and economic sanctions.

Saylor often points to the role of Bitcoin as a tool for financial empowerment in regions with unstable currencies or authoritarian regimes. For individuals living in such conditions, Bitcoin provides a way to protect their wealth and gain financial freedom. This use case is particularly relevant in countries experiencing hyperinflation, such as Venezuela and Zimbabwe.

At the same time, geopolitical tensions and economic rivalries are driving nations to diversify their reserves away from the U.S. dollar. Saylor believes that Bitcoin's neutral and decentralized nature makes it an ideal candidate for inclusion in national reserves, further boosting its global adoption and value.

Key Quotes and Interviews Supporting His Vision

Michael Saylor's $100K prediction for Bitcoin is supported by a wealth of quotes and insights he has shared in interviews, podcasts, and conferences. These statements offer a glimpse into his thought process and the reasons behind his unwavering confidence in Bitcoin's future.

One of Saylor's most memorable quotes is

"Bitcoin is the apex property of the human race. It's the first engineered monetary system that's based on a set of rules that no politician or institution can tamper with."

This statement encapsulates Saylor's belief in Bitcoin's uniqueness and its potential to revolutionize the financial system. By framing Bitcoin as an engineered solution to the problems of fiat money, Saylor highlights its technological and economic superiority.

In another interview, Saylor explained his long-term perspective on Bitcoin's value:

"The question is not whether Bitcoin will reach $100,000, but when. As more people understand its potential and adopt it, the price will naturally reflect its growing utility and scarcity."

Saylor's confidence in Bitcoin's trajectory is also evident in his discussions about its adoption curve. He often compares Bitcoin to the early days of the internet, stating:

"If you think about the internet in 1998, it was disruptive, misunderstood, and volatile. But look where it is now. Bitcoin is on the same path."

These quotes, along with many others, underscore Saylor's deep understanding of Bitcoin and his conviction that it will continue to gain value as adoption grows.

Michael J. Saylor's $100,000 prediction for Bitcoin by 2025 is more than just a bold claim; it is a vision grounded in analysis, experience, and a profound understanding of macroeconomic trends. Through his advocacy, investment strategy, and thought leadership, Saylor has become a central figure in the Bitcoin revolution, inspiring countless individuals and institutions to explore its potential. As the factors driving Bitcoin's growth continue to unfold, Saylor's forecast serves as both a roadmap and a rallying cry for those who believe in the transformative power of this digital asset.

Chapter Four: The Path to $1 Million

.Michael J. Saylor's long-term prediction of Bitcoin reaching $1 million per coin is one of his most ambitious and controversial assertions. While skeptics view such forecasts as overly optimistic or speculative, Saylor presents a compelling argument grounded in economics, history, and technology. His projection highlights Bitcoin's unique characteristics, including its fixed supply, growing demand, and comparison to traditional stores of value like gold. This chapter explores Saylor's vision for Bitcoin's path to $1 million, examining the factors he believes will drive its value to unprecedented heights.

Saylor's Long-Term Projection of Bitcoin Reaching $1M

Saylor's $1 million projection for Bitcoin reflects his belief in its potential to become the world's premier store of value. He views Bitcoin not just as a cryptocurrency but as an entirely new monetary system that addresses the shortcomings of traditional financial structures.

Saylor's thesis is based on the idea that Bitcoin will increasingly absorb the market share of other asset classes traditionally used to store wealth, such as gold, real estate, and sovereign debt. He argues that Bitcoin offers a superior alternative to these assets due to its portability, divisibility, and resistance to confiscation or devaluation.

In several interviews, Saylor has explained his rationale for the $1 million target:

1. Market Capitalization Growth: Saylor envisions Bitcoin's market capitalization surpassing $20 trillion, which would bring its price to roughly $1 million per coin. He believes this is achievable as Bitcoin gains recognition as digital gold and attracts investments from institutional players, governments, and retail investors.

2. Global Adoption: Saylor predicts that as global adoption of Bitcoin accelerates, its network effect will drive exponential growth. He compares Bitcoin to other transformative technologies, such as the internet, smartphones, and social media, which saw their value and impact skyrocket as adoption increased.

3. Fiat Currency Devaluation: Saylor often cites the ongoing devaluation of fiat currencies due to excessive money printing and inflation as a key driver of Bitcoin's long-term price appreciation. In his view, Bitcoin offers a hedge against these risks, making it an attractive option for investors seeking to preserve their purchasing power.

Saylor's $1 million projection is not tied to a specific timeline but is framed as an eventual outcome based on the continued expansion of Bitcoin's adoption and utility.

The Role of Scarcity (21 Million Cap) and Increasing Demand

At the core of Saylor's prediction is Bitcoin's fixed supply cap of 21 million coins. This built-in scarcity, enforced by Bitcoin's decentralized protocol, is a defining characteristic that sets it apart from fiat currencies and even other cryptocurrencies.

1. The Economics of Scarcity

The principle of scarcity plays a crucial role in determining the value of any asset. In traditional economics, scarcity creates value when demand exceeds supply. Saylor frequently emphasizes that Bitcoin is the first monetary system in history with a mathematically guaranteed supply cap. Unlike fiat currencies, which can be printed at will, or gold, which can be mined indefinitely, Bitcoin's supply is finite.

As of now, approximately 19.5 million Bitcoins have been mined, leaving less than 2 million yet to be created. This diminishing supply, combined with the predictable rate of issuance (halved every four years during the Bitcoin halving), creates a deflationary mechanism that contrasts sharply with the inflationary nature of fiat currencies.

2. Increasing Demand

While Bitcoin's supply is fixed, its demand continues to grow as more individuals, institutions, and governments recognize its value. Saylor identifies several factors driving this increasing demand:
Institutional Participation: Major corporations, hedge funds, and investment firms are allocating a portion of their portfolios to Bitcoin, validating its role as a legitimate asset class.

Retail Adoption: Millions of retail investors around the world are buying Bitcoin as a long-term store of value and a hedge against inflation.

Geopolitical Instability: In countries experiencing economic turmoil or authoritarian regimes, Bitcoin is becoming a lifeline for preserving wealth and ensuring financial sovereignty.

Technological Advancements: The development of layer-2 solutions like the Lightning Network and innovations in Bitcoin infrastructure are making the cryptocurrency more accessible and scalable, further boosting adoption.

As demand continues to rise and the supply remains fixed, Saylor believes that Bitcoin's value will inevitably increase, eventually reaching $1 million per coin.

Comparisons to Gold and Other Stores of Value

Saylor often frames Bitcoin as "digital gold," a phrase that encapsulates its potential to surpass gold as the preferred store of value. This comparison is central to his $1 million prediction, as it positions Bitcoin within the context of a well-established asset class.

1. Bitcoin vs. Gold

Saylor's arguments for Bitcoin's superiority over gold focus on three key attributes:

Portability: Bitcoin can be transferred instantly across the globe, whereas gold is bulky and expensive to move.

Divisibility: Bitcoin is divisible into 100 million units (satoshis), allowing for microtransactions, whereas gold is difficult to divide for small-scale transactions.

Security: Bitcoin's decentralized network ensures that it cannot be easily confiscated or counterfeited, unlike physical gold.

Gold's market capitalization of approximately $12 trillion serves as a benchmark for Saylor's Bitcoin valuation. He argues that as Bitcoin continues to gain recognition as a store of value, it will capture an increasing share of gold's market cap, eventually surpassing it.

2. Bitcoin vs. Real Estate

In addition to gold, Saylor sees Bitcoin as a superior alternative to real estate as a store of value. He points out that real estate is often illiquid, expensive to maintain, and subject to government regulation and taxation. Bitcoin, on the other hand, is highly liquid, requires no maintenance, and offers global accessibility.
Saylor predicts that as investors seek more efficient ways to store wealth, they will increasingly shift from real estate to Bitcoin, driving its price higher.

3. Bitcoin vs. Sovereign Debt

Saylor also critiques the use of sovereign debt as a store of value, particularly in an era of negative real interest rates. He argues that government bonds are becoming less attractive due to inflation and the risk of default. In contrast, Bitcoin offers a decentralized and deflationary alternative that is not tied to the fiscal policies of any nation.

In Conclusion, Michael J. Saylor's long-term prediction of Bitcoin reaching $1 million per coin is rooted in his deep understanding of economics, technology, and macroeconomic trends. By emphasizing Bitcoin's fixed supply, growing demand, and superior attributes compared to traditional stores of value, Saylor presents a compelling case for its eventual rise to this monumental price point.

While the path to $1 million may be fraught with volatility and challenges, Saylor's vision serves as a powerful reminder of Bitcoin's transformative potential. As adoption continues to expand and the world grapples with the shortcomings of fiat currencies and traditional financial systems, Bitcoin's role as the ultimate store of value becomes increasingly clear.

Saylor's prediction is not merely a numerical target but a statement of belief in the future of decentralized money and the enduring power of innovation to reshape the global economy. Whether Bitcoin ultimately reaches $1 million or not, its journey will undoubtedly leave a lasting impact on the financial landscape.

Chapter 5: Bitcoin's Volatility—A Necessary Growth Element

One of the most frequently discussed aspects of Bitcoin is its volatility. The cryptocurrency's price is known for its extreme fluctuations, which can swing dramatically within short time periods. While some investors view this volatility as a risk, Michael J. Saylor, one of Bitcoin's most prominent advocates, sees it as a necessary and even positive part of Bitcoin's evolution. In this chapter, we'll explore Saylor's perspective on Bitcoin's volatility, examine case studies of major price swings, and discuss how investors can manage risks in the Bitcoin market.

Saylor's Perspective on Volatility as an Essential Part of Bitcoin's Evolution

Michael Saylor firmly believes that Bitcoin's volatility is not something to be feared but rather a critical component of its maturation. According to Saylor, Bitcoin is still in its early stages as an asset class, and its market is still developing. Volatility, in this sense, reflects the growing pains of a new technology attempting to find its true value and integrate into the global financial system.

1. Bitcoin's Early Stage and Adoption Curve

Saylor often compares Bitcoin to emerging technologies in their infancy, such as the early days of the internet or the advent of mobile phones. He argues that as Bitcoin gains adoption and mainstream recognition, the market will become more stable. This process is natural, as assets and technologies typically experience extreme volatility in the early stages of their existence before finding a more stable equilibrium.

He believes that Bitcoin's volatility is reflective of its adoption curve: in the early stages, new ideas are tested, and markets fluctuate wildly as participants try to understand the technology's value proposition. Over time, as the user base broadens, price swings will likely become less severe.

2. Supply and Demand Dynamics

Saylor's view on volatility is also linked to Bitcoin's fixed supply and the dynamics of demand. Bitcoin's total supply is capped at 21 million, and this scarcity drives its price. As demand for Bitcoin increases, particularly from institutional investors, large movements in the market can occur. However, Saylor sees this as a sign of the asset's growing importance and recognition in the global economy.

Saylor argues that Bitcoin's volatility is a natural result of its unique characteristics, including its lack of a central issuer, limited supply, and decentralized nature. This makes it different from traditional assets such as equities, bonds, and fiat currencies, all of which are influenced by central banks or government policies. In the absence of central regulation, Bitcoin's price is driven by market participants and their collective understanding of its value. Consequently, significant volatility is to be expected during periods of price discovery.

3. Institutional and Retail Adoption Impact

Saylor also acknowledges that Bitcoin's volatility is exacerbated by its current mix of institutional and retail participants. Institutional investors tend to be more sophisticated and less reactive to short-term price swings, while retail investors may be more prone to buying and selling based on market sentiment. As institutional adoption grows, Saylor believes that Bitcoin's volatility will gradually decrease because large-scale investors typically prefer assets with lower volatility and a more predictable price trajectory.

However, Saylor also points out that this shift will take time. The market is still in the process of maturing, and until a larger number of institutional investors enter the space, Bitcoin will likely continue to experience volatility. For Saylor, this is just part of the growing process of a revolutionary technology that will ultimately change the way the world views money.

Case Studies of Major Price Swings and Their Impact on the Market

Over the years, Bitcoin has experienced several major price swings, each of which has had a significant impact on both the cryptocurrency market and the broader financial landscape. These price fluctuations are often cited as evidence of Bitcoin's volatility, but they also reveal important insights into the asset's development.

1. Bitcoin's Price Surge in 2017

One of the most notable examples of Bitcoin's volatility occurred in 2017, when the price of Bitcoin surged from around $1,000 in January to nearly $20,000 by December of that year. This dramatic increase was driven by a combination of factors, including growing media attention, increased retail interest, and speculation about Bitcoin's potential to replace traditional fiat currencies.

However, the meteoric rise in Bitcoin's price was followed by an equally dramatic crash in early 2018. By February 2018, Bitcoin's price had fallen by more than 50%, marking the start of a prolonged bear market. This event was a major point of reflection for many Bitcoin investors and was widely discussed as a cautionary tale about the risks of investing in such a volatile asset.

Despite the crash, Saylor saw the 2017 price surge and subsequent correction as part of Bitcoin's natural evolution. The market was still in its infancy, and the volatility was a reflection of a market trying to establish a true price discovery mechanism. Saylor argues that the long-term trend is more important than short-term fluctuations, and he remained confident that Bitcoin's value would continue to rise as adoption and awareness increased.

2. The 2020 Pandemic and Bitcoin's Resilience

Another major price swing occurred in 2020 when the COVID-19 pandemic led to global economic uncertainty. In March 2020, Bitcoin's price plummeted from around $9,100 to nearly $4,300 in a matter of days, following a broader market sell-off. This sharp decline was part of the widespread panic in global markets, as investors sought to liquidate assets to raise cash amid fears of an economic downturn.

However, Bitcoin's price quickly recovered, and by the end of 2020, it had surpassed its previous all-time highs. This recovery was driven by several factors, including increased institutional investment, the growing interest in Bitcoin as a hedge against inflation, and the development of more infrastructure to support Bitcoin's use and storage. Saylor viewed this recovery as a turning point for Bitcoin, highlighting its resilience in the face of market turmoil. He believes that Bitcoin's ability to recover from such steep drops is a testament to its long-term value proposition.

3. The 2021 Bull Run and Institutional Adoption

In 2021, Bitcoin experienced another significant price surge, this time driven by the institutional adoption of the cryptocurrency. In early 2021, Bitcoin's price broke through the $40,000 mark and continued to rise throughout the year, reaching an all-time high of around $64,000 in April. This rally was fueled by major institutional investments from companies like Tesla and MicroStrategy, as well as increased interest from traditional financial institutions such as banks and asset managers.

However, this bull market was also followed by another correction in the second half of 2021, with Bitcoin's price falling back down to around $30,000 in the summer before recovering again. Despite the volatility, Saylor remained optimistic about Bitcoin's long-term trajectory, believing that as more institutions entered the space and regulatory clarity improved, the market would become more stable.

Insights on Managing Risks in Bitcoin Investments

While Saylor believes that Bitcoin's volatility is an essential element of its growth, he also recognizes the importance of managing risks when investing in the cryptocurrency. For Saylor, the key to successfully navigating Bitcoin's price swings lies in a long-term perspective, proper risk management strategies, and a deep understanding of the asset's potential.

1. The Importance of Long-Term Thinking

Saylor emphasizes that Bitcoin is not a get-rich-quick asset, and short-term fluctuations should not dictate investment decisions. Instead, he advocates for a long-term investment strategy, where Bitcoin is viewed as a store of value rather than a speculative asset. According to Saylor, the price swings are part of Bitcoin's journey toward mainstream adoption, and those who hold their positions over time are likely to benefit as the asset matures.

2. Diversification and Position Sizing

While Saylor is a strong believer in Bitcoin's potential, he also advises investors to practice diversification. He recommends that investors allocate a portion of their portfolio to Bitcoin, but they should balance their exposure to the cryptocurrency with other assets to mitigate risk. Proper position sizing, where Bitcoin is viewed as part of a broader, diversified portfolio, is key to managing the risks associated with volatility.

3. Understanding the Technology

Saylor also stresses the importance of understanding Bitcoin's underlying technology. For those who truly believe in Bitcoin's long-term potential, its volatility becomes less of a concern. By understanding the fundamental principles that drive Bitcoin's value, such as its scarcity and decentralized nature, investors are better equipped to ride out the market's ups and downs.

In Conclusion, Bitcoin's volatility, while daunting at times, is a necessary and even healthy part of its evolution as an asset class. Saylor views it as an inevitable consequence of Bitcoin's journey toward mass adoption, and he remains confident that, over the long term, the cryptocurrency's value will continue to rise as it becomes a more widely accepted store of value.

For investors, understanding Bitcoin's volatility and adopting a long-term perspective is key to navigating the risks and rewards of the market. As institutional adoption increases and the market matures, Saylor believes that Bitcoin's price swings will eventually stabilize, making it a more predictable and reliable asset. Until then, the volatility serves as both a challenge and an opportunity for those who are willing to embrace it.

Chapter Six: The Institutional Revolution

In recent years, Bitcoin has undergone a significant transformation, shifting from a niche digital asset used primarily by tech enthusiasts and early adopters to a globally recognized store of value embraced by institutional investors. This chapter explores the growing institutional adoption of Bitcoin, particularly focusing on the impact of exchange-traded funds (ETFs), corporate investments, and major financial players like BlackRock and Fidelity. Additionally, we will delve into how this institutional embrace aligns with Michael Saylor's vision of Bitcoin as a digital store of value and its long-term potential in the financial ecosystem.

Analysis of Institutional Bitcoin Adoption: ETFs and Corporate Investments

Institutional adoption of Bitcoin marks one of the most significant developments in the cryptocurrency's history. Traditionally viewed as a speculative and highly volatile asset, Bitcoin is increasingly being recognized by large financial institutions as a legitimate investment vehicle. This shift has been propelled by growing demand for alternative assets, the search for inflation hedges, and the growing institutional infrastructure surrounding Bitcoin.

1. The Rise of Bitcoin ETFs

Exchange-Traded Funds (ETFs) have played a pivotal role in institutional Bitcoin adoption. ETFs offer investors a simple and regulated way to gain exposure to Bitcoin without having to directly buy, store, or manage the underlying asset. The launch of Bitcoin ETFs, particularly in the United States, has been a significant milestone in the mainstream acceptance of Bitcoin as a financial asset.
In 2021, the launch of the ProShares Bitcoin Strategy ETF (BITO) was a landmark event, as it allowed investors to gain exposure to Bitcoin futures without directly holding Bitcoin. This ETF's launch marked the first U.S. Bitcoin-linked ETF, with a price tag that surged with investor interest. The approval of Bitcoin futures ETFs signaled a broader acceptance of Bitcoin by traditional financial markets and paved the way for further financial products tied to the cryptocurrency.
Saylor, as an outspoken Bitcoin advocate, has always supported the idea of Bitcoin ETFs, understanding their potential to bridge the gap between traditional finance and the crypto world. The approval of Bitcoin ETFs by regulatory bodies like the U.S. Securities and Exchange Commission (SEC) is crucial, as it signals that Bitcoin is

gradually being recognized as a legitimate asset class. For institutional investors, ETFs provide a safe and regulated way to gain exposure to Bitcoin, and they serve as a gateway for large-scale investments into the cryptocurrency.

2. Corporate Investments in Bitcoin

Another area where institutional adoption has taken off is in corporate investments in Bitcoin. Many companies, from tech giants to traditional businesses, have started adding Bitcoin to their balance sheets as part of their treasury management strategies. Perhaps the most notable example is MicroStrategy, the business intelligence firm led by Michael Saylor himself. MicroStrategy became the first publicly traded company to adopt Bitcoin as its primary treasury reserve asset, purchasing over 120,000 BTC to date.

Other major companies followed suit, including Tesla, which made headlines in early 2021 when it announced a $1.5 billion Bitcoin purchase, signaling the carmaker's belief in Bitcoin as a store of value. Square (now Block), the payment company led by Jack Dorsey, also made substantial investments in Bitcoin, reinforcing the idea that Bitcoin is becoming an integral part of the corporate financial ecosystem.

These corporate investments represent a shift in how businesses view Bitcoin, transitioning from skepticism to recognition of its potential as a hedge against inflation and a store of value. This growing trend among companies to hold Bitcoin on their balance sheets aligns closely with Saylor's vision of Bitcoin as digital gold, offering a non-correlated, decentralized alternative to traditional cash reserves.

Saylor has often emphasized that Bitcoin is a superior treasury asset compared to fiat currencies because of its scarcity and ability to retain value over time. For corporations, Bitcoin provides an alternative to holding large amounts of cash or bonds, which are subject to inflationary pressures and low yields. By holding Bitcoin, companies can diversify their assets and protect themselves from currency devaluation, particularly in an era of rising global debt levels and uncertain monetary policies.

The Influence of Major Players like BlackRock and Fidelity

The institutional adoption of Bitcoin is not limited to corporate investments. Some of the largest asset managers and financial institutions in the world have also entered the Bitcoin market, further solidifying its status as a mainstream asset. Two such players,

BlackRock and Fidelity, have played crucial roles in driving Bitcoin adoption among institutional investors.

1. BlackRock's Involvement in Bitcoin

BlackRock, the world's largest asset management firm, made waves in 2021 when it filed with the U.S. SEC to offer Bitcoin futures trading in some of its funds. As of 2022, BlackRock launched its first Bitcoin-related fund, signaling its willingness to incorporate cryptocurrency into its portfolio. While BlackRock initially took a cautious approach toward Bitcoin, its eventual entry into the market reflects the growing acceptance of Bitcoin as an investment asset class.

BlackRock's involvement is significant because of the firm's size and influence within the investment world. As an institutional investor with over $8 trillion in assets under management, BlackRock's decisions often set the tone for the broader financial industry. By offering Bitcoin exposure to institutional clients, BlackRock legitimizes Bitcoin as an asset class and provides its clients with access to the growing crypto market. BlackRock's CEO, Larry Fink, has expressed that he sees Bitcoin as a potential "digital gold," reinforcing the idea that Bitcoin's long-term role could be as a store of value rather than a speculative asset.

2. Fidelity's Role in Bitcoin Adoption

Fidelity is another major player that has helped drive Bitcoin adoption. Fidelity has been one of the earliest institutional firms to embrace Bitcoin, providing services such as Bitcoin custodial solutions, trading platforms, and research for institutional clients. In fact, Fidelity has been offering Bitcoin custody services to institutional investors since 2018, making it one of the first large financial firms to recognize the potential of digital assets.

Fidelity's CEO, Abigail Johnson, has been a vocal supporter of Bitcoin and blockchain technology. Under her leadership, Fidelity has made substantial investments in cryptocurrency-related businesses and has actively worked to provide its clients with access to Bitcoin and other digital assets. Fidelity's long-term vision aligns closely with Saylor's perspective on Bitcoin's role as a store of value. Like Saylor, Fidelity views Bitcoin as a deflationary asset that offers an alternative to traditional fiat currencies and an efficient way to preserve wealth over time.

Fidelity's influence in the financial world cannot be overstated. The firm's recognition of Bitcoin's value and its willingness to invest heavily in Bitcoin infrastructure have helped pave the way for other institutions to follow suit. As more financial institutions begin to offer Bitcoin services, it becomes increasingly clear that Bitcoin is no longer a fringe asset but a legitimate part of the financial system.

How Institutions Align with Saylor's Vision

The growing institutional adoption of Bitcoin is a development that aligns closely with Michael Saylor's vision for the cryptocurrency. Saylor has consistently argued that Bitcoin's role as a store of value is central to its future, and he believes that institutional investors will be key to driving its long-term growth. As large institutions like BlackRock, Fidelity, and major corporations like MicroStrategy and Tesla embrace Bitcoin, they validate Saylor's thesis that Bitcoin is an asset worth holding as a reserve.

1. Institutional Trust in Bitcoin as a Store of Value

Saylor has often likened Bitcoin to gold, emphasizing its scarcity and the fact that it is not subject to the inflationary pressures of fiat currencies. Bitcoin's fixed supply, capped at 21 million coins, makes it an attractive alternative to traditional forms of money, which can be printed at will by central banks. For institutions, this scarcity is a key selling point. Bitcoin's ability to retain value over time and act as a hedge against inflation aligns with the financial goals of institutional investors, who seek assets that can preserve wealth in the long term.

2. The Future of Bitcoin in Traditional Finance

Saylor's vision for Bitcoin goes beyond its use as an investment vehicle. He believes that Bitcoin will eventually become the primary global reserve currency, replacing fiat currencies as the world's standard of value. The growing institutional adoption of Bitcoin is a critical step toward realizing this vision. As institutions increasingly embrace Bitcoin, it becomes more entrenched in the global financial ecosystem, bringing us closer to the day when Bitcoin may serve as the backbone of the global economy.

3. Institutional Support for Bitcoin's Technological Development

Saylor has also highlighted that institutional investment in Bitcoin is not just about financial returns. Large financial institutions like Fidelity and BlackRock are actively investing in the infrastructure and technology that will support Bitcoin's growth. This includes services such as custodial solutions, trading platforms, and blockchain technology research. These investments help ensure that Bitcoin will be able to scale and remain secure as its user base grows.

In Conclusion, the growing institutional adoption of Bitcoin is a testament to the cryptocurrency's increasing legitimacy in the global financial system. Through the launch of Bitcoin ETFs, corporate investments, and the involvement of major financial players like BlackRock and Fidelity, Bitcoin is gaining acceptance as a store of value and an alternative asset class. This institutional revolution aligns closely with Michael Saylor's vision of Bitcoin as a digital gold, and it signals that Bitcoin's journey to becoming a mainstream financial asset is well underway.

As more institutions recognize the potential of Bitcoin, its price stability and mainstream acceptance are likely to improve, ultimately leading to greater adoption worldwide. For Saylor, the involvement of institutions is a sign that Bitcoin is fulfilling its purpose as a global store of value, and he remains optimistic about its long-term prospects.

Chapter Seven: The Future of Bitcoin Under Global Changes

As the global political and economic landscape continues to evolve, Bitcoin's role as a decentralized, borderless asset has become more significant. The cryptocurrency has long been seen as a hedge against inflation, an alternative store of value, and a potential solution for countries grappling with economic instability or currency devaluation. In this chapter, we will explore Bitcoin's potential in a rapidly changing world, focusing on the impact of global changes, U.S. crypto policies, and the increasing trends of global adoption. Additionally, we will examine how these developments align with Michael Saylor's predictions and his long-term vision for Bitcoin as a store of value.

Bitcoin's Potential in a Changing Political and Economic Landscape

Bitcoin's decentralized nature gives it a unique advantage in the face of global political and economic changes. As traditional financial systems become more complex and often strained, Bitcoin offers an alternative that is free from government control, centralized monetary policies, and traditional banking systems. The cryptocurrency is often described as "digital gold" due to its scarcity, security, and independence from inflationary pressures, making it an attractive option in times of political and economic uncertainty.

1. Bitcoin as a Hedge Against Inflation

One of the key reasons Bitcoin is gaining attention in today's volatile economic environment is its potential to serve as a hedge against inflation. As central banks continue to print money and accumulate debt, many traditional fiat currencies are facing devaluation. Governments around the world have resorted to printing more money in response to global crises, such as the COVID-19 pandemic, leading to an increase in inflation and a reduction in the purchasing power of fiat currencies.

Bitcoin, on the other hand, has a fixed supply of 21 million coins, which means that its value is not susceptible to the same inflationary pressures. This scarcity makes it an appealing alternative to fiat currencies, particularly in regions where inflation is rampant, such as Venezuela and Argentina. For countries experiencing hyperinflation, Bitcoin offers a way for citizens to protect their wealth and transfer value without relying on unstable local currencies.

Michael Saylor, a vocal proponent of Bitcoin, has repeatedly emphasized this point. He argues that Bitcoin is superior to traditional currencies because it is not subject to inflation or central bank policies. Saylor believes that Bitcoin's ability to retain its value over time is one of the primary reasons that institutional investors and corporations are increasingly turning to it as a store of value.

2. Bitcoin and Political Instability

Political instability, whether it's the threat of war, regime change, or economic sanctions, often results in a loss of confidence in national currencies. In these circumstances, people look for alternative ways to store and transfer wealth. Bitcoin, due to its decentralized nature, can serve as a lifeline for individuals in politically unstable countries, offering a safe, borderless, and secure method of storing value and conducting transactions.

In countries facing political upheaval, Bitcoin has already begun to play a significant role in preserving wealth. For instance, in nations like Iran and Russia, where sanctions have limited access to traditional financial systems, Bitcoin has provided an avenue for citizens and businesses to transact internationally and store value outside the reach of their governments. The ability to access Bitcoin without the need for intermediaries, such as banks, is an attractive feature for individuals in politically volatile regions.

Saylor's vision aligns with the idea that Bitcoin could ultimately act as a global reserve asset, functioning as a stable store of value even in the most challenging political environments. As the world becomes increasingly interconnected and unstable, the demand for Bitcoin could rise as people seek a reliable, decentralized alternative to national currencies that can be easily transferred and stored.

3. The Impact of Geopolitical Tensions

Geopolitical tensions, including trade wars, territorial disputes, and military conflicts, also have the potential to drive Bitcoin adoption. As countries find themselves embroiled in conflicts that disrupt trade or destabilize national currencies, Bitcoin's ability to function as a borderless and immutable asset becomes increasingly valuable.

The ongoing tensions between the U.S. and China, for example, have made it clear that reliance on traditional financial systems could be risky for countries seeking independence from the influence of foreign powers. Bitcoin provides an alternative to the traditional dollar-based financial system, offering countries and individuals a method of storing value and transferring assets free from the control of any single nation-state.

Saylor, who has been a staunch advocate of Bitcoin as a "non-sovereign" asset, sees the geopolitical landscape as another reason why Bitcoin is poised for continued growth. As global tensions rise, Bitcoin may become more attractive to both individual investors and national governments who seek to protect themselves from external political risks.

How New U.S. Crypto Policies Could Affect Saylor's Predictions

As Bitcoin continues to gain traction in the financial world, regulatory frameworks are beginning to take shape in countries around the world. In the United States, the crypto market has seen significant attention from lawmakers and regulators, with debates centering on how to handle digital assets like Bitcoin. The evolving regulatory landscape in the U.S. will have a major impact on Bitcoin's future, particularly in terms of its adoption by institutional investors and its role in the global economy.

1. The Role of Regulatory Clarity

For institutional investors to fully embrace Bitcoin, they need clear and consistent regulatory guidelines. While Bitcoin has already seen significant corporate adoption, uncertainty surrounding regulatory policies has prevented some investors from fully committing to the asset. This is particularly true in the United States, where the lack of a comprehensive regulatory framework has created an environment of uncertainty.

However, recent developments suggest that the U.S. is moving toward a more defined regulatory approach to crypto. The U.S. Securities and Exchange Commission (SEC) has been taking a more active role in overseeing digital assets, and lawmakers are beginning to introduce bills aimed at clarifying the legal status of Bitcoin and other cryptocurrencies. These efforts to regulate the crypto market could help institutional investors feel more confident in adopting Bitcoin, which aligns with Saylor's vision of Bitcoin as a legitimate and trusted store of value.

2. The Potential Impact of Bitcoin ETFs and Spot Market Regulations

One of the key areas where U.S. crypto policies could have a significant impact is the approval and regulation of Bitcoin exchange-traded funds (ETFs). The approval of Bitcoin ETFs by the SEC would open the floodgates for institutional capital, allowing more traditional investors to gain exposure to Bitcoin without directly purchasing and holding the asset. The regulatory approval of Bitcoin ETFs would likely increase demand for Bitcoin and further solidify its position as a mainstream investment asset.

Additionally, regulations that govern the spot market for Bitcoin, including how it is traded and taxed, will also play a critical role in shaping the future of Bitcoin in the U.S. Clear and fair taxation policies, as well as transparent rules surrounding the buying and selling of Bitcoin, will encourage more investors to enter the market, driving up both adoption and the price of the asset.

Saylor's predictions for Bitcoin's long-term value are closely tied to the regulatory environment in the U.S. As more clarity emerges around crypto policies, Saylor believes that institutional adoption will surge, driving the price of Bitcoin upward and reinforcing his vision of Bitcoin as a safe haven asset.

3. Geopolitical Influence on U.S. Crypto Policies

The global race to regulate cryptocurrencies is not limited to the United States. As countries like China and the European Union establish their own regulatory frameworks, the U.S. will likely face increased pressure to develop policies that protect its financial system while also fostering innovation in the crypto space. How the U.S. government decides to regulate Bitcoin will have significant implications for Saylor's predictions. If the U.S. embraces Bitcoin and positions itself as a leader in crypto adoption, it could accelerate the growth of Bitcoin, as institutional investors look to capitalize on the opportunities the cryptocurrency offers.

Global Adoption Trends and Their Alignment with Saylor's Foresight

Around the world, Bitcoin is gaining traction as more people, institutions, and governments recognize its potential as a store of value. In many emerging markets, Bitcoin's use as a hedge against inflation, a means of financial inclusion, and a tool for remittances is rapidly growing. This global trend aligns closely with Michael Saylor's vision of Bitcoin as a reserve asset that transcends national borders and central banks.

1. Emerging Markets and Financial Inclusion

In emerging markets, Bitcoin is playing a significant role in providing financial services to people who are underserved or excluded from the traditional banking system. In countries with limited access to banks or where inflation has devalued national currencies, Bitcoin offers a means to store wealth and make cross-border transactions without the need for intermediaries. For instance, in countries like Nigeria and Turkey, Bitcoin has become an essential tool for people seeking to protect their wealth from hyperinflation.

Saylor's vision of Bitcoin as a borderless, decentralized asset aligns perfectly with the financial needs of these emerging markets. As more people in these regions adopt Bitcoin, the cryptocurrency's role as a global store of value will continue to grow, reinforcing Saylor's belief that Bitcoin has the potential to replace traditional fiat currencies over time.

2. Global Institutional Adoption

As institutional investors around the world continue to embrace Bitcoin, the global adoption trend aligns with Saylor's forecast of Bitcoin reaching significant value in the coming years. From major financial institutions to national governments, Bitcoin is steadily being recognized as a legitimate and valuable asset. This global shift towards Bitcoin adoption reinforces Saylor's thesis that Bitcoin will continue to gain in value as more institutions recognize its potential.

In conclusion, Bitcoin's future is intrinsically tied to the political, economic, and regulatory changes taking place globally. With its potential to serve as a hedge against inflation, a tool for financial inclusion, and a decentralized store of value, Bitcoin is increasingly becoming an essential asset in a world of growing uncertainty. Michael Saylor's predictions for Bitcoin's future are aligned with these global trends, and as more institutions and governments adopt Bitcoin, his vision for the cryptocurrency's role in the financial system is likely to come to fruition

Chapter Eight: Criticism and Alternative Views

Michael Saylor's predictions for Bitcoin, particularly his forecasts for the cryptocurrency's price and its eventual adoption as a global store of value, have garnered significant attention. While many investors, entrepreneurs, and institutions have rallied behind Saylor's bullish outlook, there are also notable critics who have expressed skepticism about Bitcoin's long-term viability. These alternative views are rooted in concerns about Bitcoin's inherent volatility, regulatory hurdles, its environmental impact, and the possibility of competing technologies overtaking it in the future. In this chapter, we'll explore the skepticism surrounding Saylor's predictions, the bearish perspectives on Bitcoin's future, and how the balance between optimism and caution can help investors navigate the evolving cryptocurrency landscape.

Addressing Skepticism Surrounding Saylor's Predictions

Michael Saylor has been one of the most vocal proponents of Bitcoin, frequently declaring that the cryptocurrency is poised to replace gold and become the world's dominant store of value. His company,

MicroStrategy, has made significant investments in Bitcoin, and Saylor himself has been an outspoken advocate for the asset. Despite the enthusiasm surrounding his predictions, many critics have raised concerns about the plausibility of these claims, questioning whether Bitcoin can truly achieve the levels of adoption and price growth that Saylor envisions.

1. Bitcoin's Volatility

One of the primary criticisms of Bitcoin is its volatility. The cryptocurrency has experienced massive price fluctuations, with dramatic swings in value over short periods of time. For instance, Bitcoin's price surged to nearly $70,000 in late 2021, only to plummet to under $20,000 in mid-2022. Such volatility has led many skeptics to question whether Bitcoin can ever achieve the stability necessary to serve as a reliable store of value, as Saylor predicts.

Critics argue that Bitcoin's volatility makes it too risky to be considered a safe haven asset or a legitimate store of value. Unlike gold, which has a long history of being a stable store of value, Bitcoin's price can be influenced by a range of unpredictable factors, including market sentiment, regulatory developments, and technological advancements. Many investors prefer traditional assets that are less susceptible to wild price fluctuations, particularly in uncertain economic times.

In response to these criticisms, Saylor and other Bitcoin proponents argue that volatility is an inherent part of Bitcoin's growth process. They point to the cryptocurrency's early years, when it was valued at mere cents, as evidence of how volatility is part of Bitcoin's maturation. Saylor often emphasizes that Bitcoin's volatility will decrease over time as adoption increases and its market cap grows, similar to the way that gold's price has become more stable over centuries.

2. Regulatory Uncertainty

Another major source of skepticism surrounding Saylor's Bitcoin predictions is the uncertainty surrounding global regulatory frameworks. Governments and financial institutions are still grappling with how to classify and regulate Bitcoin, and many countries have taken a cautious or adversarial stance toward the cryptocurrency. The lack of clear regulatory guidelines in major economies like the United States and the European Union has led to concerns about Bitcoin's future.

Skeptics argue that governments could take actions to restrict or ban Bitcoin if it becomes too large or threatens the dominance of national currencies. Some experts warn that Bitcoin's decentralized nature could pose a threat to traditional financial systems, and governments may impose strict regulations or even prohibit the use of Bitcoin in favor of central bank digital currencies (CBDCs). Furthermore, concerns about money laundering, tax evasion, and financial crime have led to calls for increased regulation of the crypto market.

Saylor, however, remains optimistic about Bitcoin's regulatory future. He believes that the cryptocurrency will ultimately benefit from clear and consistent regulation, which will help legitimize it in the eyes of institutional investors. He points to the increasing number of regulatory bodies that are working to provide clarity on Bitcoin's legal status, as well as the growing acceptance of the asset by financial institutions, as signs that the regulatory landscape will eventually become more favorable.

3. Environmental Impact

Bitcoin's energy consumption has been another significant point of criticism. The process of mining Bitcoin, known as proof-of-work, requires a vast amount of computational power and energy. In fact, Bitcoin's energy consumption has been compared to that of entire countries, with critics arguing that the environmental impact of Bitcoin mining is unsustainable.

Environmentalists have raised concerns about the carbon footprint of Bitcoin mining, particularly in regions where the electricity used for mining comes from fossil fuels.

The environmental debate has become a major point of contention, with some arguing that the benefits of Bitcoin as a financial innovation do not outweigh the ecological costs.

Saylor and other Bitcoin proponents acknowledge the environmental concerns but argue that Bitcoin can be powered by renewable energy sources. Saylor has pointed to the growing trend of miners using solar, hydroelectric, and wind power to mine Bitcoin, arguing that this shift toward sustainable energy will reduce the ecological impact of the cryptocurrency. Additionally, he believes that Bitcoin's ability to offer a decentralized and borderless financial system is worth the environmental trade-offs, particularly in comparison to traditional financial systems, which also consume significant resources.

Exploring Bearish Perspectives on Bitcoin's Future

While Saylor remains firmly optimistic about Bitcoin's future, there are a number of bearish perspectives that offer a more cautionary view of the cryptocurrency. These critics believe that Bitcoin faces significant challenges that could prevent it from realizing Saylor's vision of becoming a global store of value.

1. Competition from Other Cryptocurrencies

One of the primary concerns among Bitcoin's critics is the rise of competing cryptocurrencies that may outperform Bitcoin in the future. While Bitcoin is the first and most well-known cryptocurrency, it is not the only one. Other digital assets, such as Ethereum, Binance Coin, and Solana, have gained popularity due to their unique features, such as faster transaction times, lower fees, and more scalable blockchain technologies.

Critics argue that Bitcoin's dominance in the cryptocurrency market is not guaranteed, and that new technologies could surpass Bitcoin's capabilities. For example, Ethereum's shift to a proof-of-stake consensus mechanism, which is more energy-efficient than Bitcoin's proof-of-work, could make it a more attractive option for investors and developers. Additionally, the rise of central bank digital currencies (CBDCs) could reduce demand for decentralized cryptocurrencies like Bitcoin.

2. Technological Limitations

Another concern for Bitcoin's future is its scalability. While Bitcoin has proven to be a secure and reliable digital asset, its blockchain is limited in terms of transaction throughput. The Bitcoin network can only process a relatively small number of transactions per second compared to traditional payment systems like

Visa or Mastercard, which can handle thousands of transactions per second.

Critics argue that Bitcoin's scalability issues could hinder its adoption as a global payment system or a widely used store of value. Although solutions like the Lightning Network have been proposed to address these limitations, skeptics believe that Bitcoin's technological constraints may eventually be its downfall.

3. Market Sentiment and Speculation

Some critics argue that Bitcoin's price is primarily driven by speculation and market sentiment, rather than its inherent utility or value as a store of value. They point to the volatile swings in Bitcoin's price as evidence that the cryptocurrency is more of a speculative asset than a stable investment. In this view, Bitcoin's price could collapse if investor sentiment shifts or if a major market correction occurs.

Balancing Optimism with Caution

While Bitcoin's potential is undeniable, it is important for investors to balance optimism with caution. Saylor's bold predictions for Bitcoin's future are based on a number of factors, including increased institutional adoption, regulatory clarity, and the growing demand for decentralized financial systems. However, the criticisms and alternative views outlined in this chapter highlight the risks and challenges that Bitcoin faces in the coming years.

For investors, it is essential to consider both the potential rewards and the risks associated with Bitcoin. While Saylor's vision of Bitcoin becoming a dominant store of value may come to fruition, it is important to acknowledge the inherent uncertainties and challenges that the cryptocurrency faces. By maintaining a balanced perspective, investors can better navigate the volatile and rapidly evolving world of Bitcoin and other digital assets.

In Conclusion, Bitcoin's future is filled with both promise and uncertainty. Michael Saylor's predictions for Bitcoin's price and role in the global financial system are ambitious and optimistic, but they are not without their critics. Addressing skepticism surrounding Bitcoin's volatility, regulatory uncertainty, and environmental impact is crucial for understanding the cryptocurrency's potential. By balancing optimism with caution, investors can make informed decisions about Bitcoin's place in the future of finance.

Conclusion

Michael Saylor's view of Bitcoin is not confined to its potential price or its role in financial markets. Beyond the numbers and price predictions, Saylor sees Bitcoin as a transformative technology with the power to reshape not only the financial world but also the broader global economy. For Saylor, Bitcoin represents more than just an investment opportunity or an alternative to fiat currencies. It is a paradigm shift, a new way of thinking about money, value, and the entire structure of global finance. In this conclusion, we'll explore Saylor's broader philosophy on Bitcoin, examining how he envisions its transformative role in the digital economy, and reflect on the significance of his predictions and vision for the future.

Saylor's Broader Philosophy on Bitcoin as a Transformative Technology

At the heart of Michael Saylor's philosophy on Bitcoin is the belief that the cryptocurrency represents a fundamental shift in the way humanity conceptualizes and interacts with money. Saylor has frequently compared Bitcoin to early technological innovations like the internet, mobile phones, and personal computers. Just as these innovations revolutionized communication, commerce, and daily life, Bitcoin has the potential to revolutionize how we store and transfer value.

Saylor's philosophy is rooted in the concept of Bitcoin as a "monetary revolution" that challenges the traditional financial system. He often frames Bitcoin as a response to the weaknesses of the existing financial infrastructure, particularly the issues associated with fiat currencies and central banking systems. In this regard, Saylor views Bitcoin not just as an investment vehicle but as a fundamental rethinking of how value should be stored and transmitted in an increasingly digital world.

1. The Case for Bitcoin as Digital Gold

One of Saylor's most persistent beliefs is that Bitcoin is the "digital gold" of the future. Gold has long been seen as a store of value, providing a hedge against inflation and currency devaluation. However, gold has several limitations that make it impractical in the modern world: it is difficult to store and transport, it is susceptible to theft and fraud, and it is not easily divisible. Bitcoin, by contrast, addresses all of these limitations while offering a secure, borderless, and easily transferable asset.

In Saylor's vision, Bitcoin's role as digital gold goes beyond its potential as a store of value. Bitcoin represents a new form of money that operates outside of the control of central banks and governments. As a decentralized digital asset with a fixed supply of 21 million coins, Bitcoin is immune to inflationary policies that can devalue traditional currencies. Saylor believes that this scarcity, combined with its digital nature, makes Bitcoin an ideal store of value in a world where inflation and currency devaluation are ongoing concerns.

2. The Importance of Decentralization

Central to Saylor's philosophy on Bitcoin is the concept of decentralization. In contrast to traditional financial systems, which rely on centralized institutions like banks and governments, Bitcoin operates on a decentralized peer-to-peer network. This decentralization allows for a more transparent and efficient system of transferring value without the need for intermediaries.

Saylor sees decentralization as one of Bitcoin's most powerful features, not just from a technical perspective but also from a philosophical one. By removing the need for trusted intermediaries, Bitcoin gives individuals and businesses greater autonomy over their financial transactions. This, in turn, could reduce the reliance on centralized institutions, such as banks and governments, that have historically controlled the flow of money and value.

The decentralized nature of Bitcoin also aligns with Saylor's broader belief in the democratization of financial systems. In his view, Bitcoin offers a more equitable financial infrastructure, where people can access the same financial tools and opportunities regardless of their geographic location or socioeconomic status. This vision of financial inclusion is a key component of Saylor's broader philosophy on Bitcoin as a transformative technology.

3. Bitcoin's Potential as a Hedge Against Geopolitical Risks

Another key aspect of Saylor's broader vision for Bitcoin is its potential as a hedge against geopolitical risks. In a world where global economic systems are increasingly interconnected, events like trade wars, financial crises, and political instability can have far-reaching consequences. Saylor believes that Bitcoin's decentralized nature and its immunity to government control make it a safe haven asset during times of geopolitical uncertainty.

Saylor has often pointed to countries experiencing economic instability such as Venezuela, Argentina, and Zimbabwe as examples of how Bitcoin can serve as a lifeline for individuals seeking to preserve their wealth in times of crisis. In these countries, hyperinflation and currency devaluation have made traditional forms of savings and wealth preservation virtually worthless. Bitcoin, on the other hand, offers a portable, secure, and non-governmental alternative that can be used to store value across borders.

By positioning Bitcoin as a global hedge against geopolitical risks, Saylor underscores his belief that Bitcoin's potential goes far beyond its role as a speculative asset. He sees it as a global solution to problems that affect millions of people worldwide, particularly those in countries where the financial system is fragile or inefficient.

Final Thoughts on Saylor's Predictions and Their Significance in the Digital Economy

Michael Saylor's predictions for Bitcoin's future have been bold and ambitious, but they are grounded in a broader philosophical vision for how Bitcoin can shape the future of the digital economy. Saylor's belief that Bitcoin will reach $100,000 by 2025 and eventually surpass $1 million is not just based on price charts and market trends; it is tied to his larger vision of Bitcoin as a transformative force in the global financial system.

In Saylor's view, Bitcoin represents the next logical step in the evolution of money. It is a form of money that is not subject to the whims of central banks, governments, or traditional financial institutions. It is a form of money that is global, borderless, and secure—qualities that make it uniquely suited to the demands of an increasingly digital and interconnected world.

Saylor's predictions are also a reflection of his confidence in Bitcoin's long-term potential. Unlike traditional financial markets, where asset prices are often driven by short-term market sentiment and speculative behavior, Saylor believes that Bitcoin's value will be determined by its long-term utility and its ability to solve real-world problems. Whether it's serving as a store of value, a medium of exchange, or a hedge against inflation and geopolitical risks, Saylor's vision for Bitcoin is rooted in the belief that its transformative potential will ultimately be realized as adoption grows.

At the same time, Saylor's optimism is tempered by a recognition of the risks involved in investing in Bitcoin. The cryptocurrency market is still in its early stages, and Bitcoin's price can be highly volatile. Saylor himself has acknowledged that Bitcoin's path to mainstream adoption will not be without challenges, including regulatory hurdles, technological developments, and competition from other cryptocurrencies. However, he remains confident that Bitcoin's long-term value proposition will eventually prevail.

In the context of the digital economy, Saylor's predictions hold significant implications. As Bitcoin continues to gain traction among institutional investors and governments, its role as a financial asset and a store of value will become increasingly important. Saylor's vision for Bitcoin is not just about its price or its market cap; it is about the broader shift that Bitcoin represents in the way we think about money, wealth, and value. In this sense, Bitcoin is not just a financial asset, it is a transformative technology that has the potential to reshape the entire economic landscape.

In conclusion, Michael Saylor's philosophy on Bitcoin extends far beyond numbers and price forecasts. His vision of Bitcoin as a transformative technology capable of revolutionizing the financial system, democratizing access to financial tools, and serving as a hedge against geopolitical risks is what sets him apart as a leading advocate for the cryptocurrency. Whether or not his predictions come to fruition, Saylor's broader philosophy on Bitcoin will likely continue to influence the way we think about money and finance in the digital age. As Bitcoin continues to evolve, Saylor's vision will remain a crucial part of the ongoing conversation about the future of the global economy.

www.ingramcontent.com/pod-product-compliance
Lightning Source LLC
Chambersburg PA
CBHW071106240526
45469CB00006BD/2358